BATTLE FEAR AND WIN

A 30-DAY DEVOTIONAL FOR THE FEARFUL AT HEART

HAROLD "MARTY" ZIMMERMAN III

Publisher—eGenCo

Generation Culture Transformation
Specializing in publishing for generation culture change

eGenCo
824 Tallow Hill Road
Chambersburg, PA 17202, USA
Phone: 717-461-3436
Email: info@egen.co
Website: www.egen.co

facebook.com/egenbooks
twitter.com/egen_co
youtube.com/egenpub
pinterest.com/eGenDMP
instagram.com/egen.co

Cover photography by Marty Zimmerman

Library of Congress Cataloging-in-Publication Data
Library of Congress Control Number: 2020909518

ISBN:	978-1-68019-013-7	Paperback
	978-1-68019-014-4	eBook
	978-1-68019-015-1	eBook

Printed in the United States of America

DEDICATION

I dedicate this book to my Mom and Dad, who have been stalwart supporters of me for as long as I can remember. They have been pillars I can lean on, and I am grateful that God gave them to me as my parents. Mom and Dad, thank you for encouraging me to pursue my dreams, and for helping me launch this project. You have played such a vital role in my recovery, and in my life. Thank you for the unconditional love you have offered me and helping me stay focused on Jesus while on this grand journey.

–Zimmie

Do not be anxious about anything, but in everything, by prayer and petition, with thanksgiving, present your requests to God. And the peace of God, which transcends all understanding, will guard your hearts and your minds in Christ Jesus
(Philippians 4:6-7).

TABLE OF CONTENTS

INTRODUCTION

All my life I have been anxious, from a small boy to the man I am today. I suppose you could describe me as a professional worrier. In my younger days I worried about school. I feared doing poorly on assignments. I feared failure. I feared being disciplined. I feared giving the wrong answer in class. Highly self-conscious, I have always struggled with self-confidence, at least to some degree. I tend to be a people pleaser who values the opinion of others, even strangers. Truth is, I come from a long line of worriers. Perhaps the same is true of you.

I have written this book not as a medical expert, or someone who is adept in psychology or counseling, but as someone who has suffered numerous panic attacks of varying degrees of intensity and walked through some dark and gloomy seasons. I make no claim to have overcome Anxiety as I still wrestle with it some days. Nor is this a book that promotes a multi-step process for ejecting Anxiety from one's mind by thinking happy, cheerful, and positive thoughts. What I offer to you here is a portion of my personal story, an account of how Anxiety has worked against me, and what I have found in my Christian faith that has equipped me to war against it.

We all suffer from Anxiety in some way. Men and women, young and old; we all have fears, concerns, troubles. In case you haven't noticed, the world is ruled by Fear.

News outlets spanning the globe churn out one fearful headline after another. We hear rumors and read attention-grabbing headlines that immediately play on our emotions and fill our minds with questions. We worry about crime, and about natural disasters; we worry about our families, our neighborhoods, and our communities. We worry about employment, money, and our health. The list goes on and on, and it is a very personal list. What bothers me may not bother you. What you lose sleep over may never cross my mind. We can all relate to this, though. Our subconscious minds (at least) are always busy compiling lists of our worries and trying to address each one. Often, we do not even realize how worry has overworked our minds until we lie down to sleep and find that our brains will not simply switch off. We lie in bed tossing and turning as our minds obsess over a particular issue. It is not always easy to pinpoint the problem. Sometimes it requires thinking back over the course of the day, reviewing the stops we made, and the interactions we had with others. In a tedious fashion, we comb our way through the tangle of events, conversations, and activities—sometimes for hours—before identifying the sore spot.

After finishing college, I weighed my options: What was I to do? Where was I to go? Because I had nothing lined up, I grew anxious and angry with myself for not thinking through the next step. My college friends were off to graduate school, leaving for seminary, or moving away to accept distant job offers. As for me, I eventually headed back home to Mom and Dad in my hometown of Greencastle, Pennsylvania. A short time later I found myself a part-time job at a small, family-owned grocery store. Then, in the spring of 2011, I was accepted by Shippensburg University to enroll in a master's degree program in applied history. I had long dreamed of working in a museum or with the National Park Service, educating people about historical events and the people involved. Finally, I felt like I had my feet on the ground, running towards a future that would satisfy me.

All my excitement, plans, and daily routines came to a screeching and traumatic halt on March 7, 2013, when, at the age of twenty-five, I suffered a hemorrhagic stroke due to a birth defect, something known as a brain AVM. Looking back, there is no question that God performed a series of miracles that day in preserving my life. He saved me. All the necessary people were in place, experts in their respective fields. Because of my critical condition, I was airlifted to the Hershey Medical Center, and underwent an emergency craniotomy. The remainder of 2013 was a tumultuous jumble full of heartache and new levels of Anxiety such as I had never known. By year's end I had endured five surgical procedures and six weeks of hospitalization. I wrote a book detailing the events surrounding that day in March of 2013 and my experiences through the middle of 2014. *Life Interrupted: The Story of a Young Stroke Survivor*, was my first published book. However, it only covers my journey to a certain extent. This current book continues that account, diving into my post-stroke world.

In the aftermath of the interruption, I began to notice the emergence of new giants on my horizon; terrible-looking, ghastly creatures that would move to confront me, oppose me, confine me, try and convince me that I would be safer living life behind closed doors. Can you relate to that? Have you ever wondered, considering how frightening and unpredictable the world is, whether you might be better off becoming a recluse and hiding safely behind the four walls of your house? However tempting that seems sometimes, it is an unacceptable proposition for me, and I think it should be to you as well.

Fear's aim is to isolate you, ostracize you, belittle you; to make you feel powerless in a great big world. But God has a different plan for you. He has a purpose for you, and you do not have to sacrifice that purpose for the sake of appeasing Fear in exchange for a short-term peace. Anyone who has struggled with Anxiety, anyone who is prone to worrying, knows that Fear is a fickle master. You compromise over one issue, then another something appears and peeks out to garner your attention. You cut down one weed, and a dozen more grow up to take its place. It is not enough to just cut it down; you must dig up the roots. If your house is falling down, you don't think about painting a room or hanging new curtains. You have to address the foundation; you have to correct the structure. You may be quite adept at wearing masks, hiding what is truly bubbling underneath the surface, but at some point you must face reality and deal with those underlying issues. A wound untreated will fester and lead to infection and a more critical condition.

So, come along on this journey with me as I unpack more of my own story and share more about the fears I have faced and have combatted in my life so far. I will also reserve space for poems I have written over the past three years or so that focus on Anxiety and Fear. My struggles have inspired a number of compositions. Writing has helped me to process, to vent, to give voice to my inner angst, to rediscover some profound truths that I have known but lost sight of for one reason or another. Over the next thirty days we will take a look at Fear and dissect it. We will review questions, formulate responses, and look to God's Word for revelation about how we can overcome Fear. Although God sometimes does release persons immediately and deliver them from Fear in the span of a moment, more often, especially to gain breakthrough, win a prize, or reach a positive result, we must undergo a process. A process implies that an investment must be made over the course of time; it requires a prolonged effort. This is a place for candidness. This is a place for you and me to give voice to those closely held fears, to look at them from a different vantage point, while in the presence of our Heavenly Father.

I realize that each person wrestles with Anxiety differently. Some have much deeper, much sharper engagements. There are different remedies available when dealing with Anxiety. You will have to consider the options and pick what you consider the best fit for you. There is no shame in reaching out to others for help. Often, a listening ear is just the thing needed. I know that has helped me immensely in my own battle. I realize, though, that some may need a counselor or a therapist, others, a medication of some sort. No judgement from me; no condemnation. What we can agree on, though, is that to live afraid, to live in Fear of invisible threats, is no way to live. Identifying this and moving away from it is the right move to make. So, as long as you are willing to leave

Anxiety behind, then I say we are on the same page. I hope that this simple, daily devotional will encourage you, empower you, and bless you. Let us invite God to lead the way on this short sojourn. May He help us locate the roots of the issue and give us courage enough to dig them up. May He help us dismantle the walls we have built to keep others out. May His light bring revelation, clarity, and ultimately, freedom from the monsters that lurk in our souls, in our imaginations, and in our past. Let us expel them and ask Him to fill us with a greater degree of love, a greater capacity to love. We are more than our fears, and we need to look beyond those mislabels if we wish to live a life of influence, where we connect with others and operate in power and authority given us by Jesus.

Marty Zimmerman III

a.k.a. HMZ3

DAY ONE

I can clearly recall when I was in elementary school, how nervous I always got before stepping onto the school bus. Every day my mom walked with me to the bus stop, and every day my belly felt like I had swallowed a dozen fluttering butterflies. Beginning in preschool I had experienced separation anxiety, so on these daily walks to the bus stop, I almost always latched tightly onto Mom's hand. Strangely, I cannot remember having a reason for why I was so reluctant to leave her side; I had friends and I enjoyed playing and learning. Yet, for some reason, I was afraid of being away from her, of being alone and on my own. Do you have any similar early memories of fearful situations, or things you worried about a lot?

Since reaching adulthood I have learned that my mom is a worrier, as is her mom (my Grandma), and as was her grandmother (my Great Grandma Baer). So, I come from a long line of worriers. I guess you could say it comes naturally for me. How about you? Do you or anyone else in your immediate or extended family struggle with Anxiety? What about family members of previous generations? If so, let me encourage you with something I have found to be true in my own life: Generational curses and afflictions can be broken in the name of Jesus. What was inherited from previous generations does not have to be received. You can break the cycle.

DAY TWO

I always worried as a student, from preschool all the way through graduate school. Although I struggled with mathematics, I excelled as a student—and as a worrier. I did well, but despite numerous awards and accolades I received, I often worried that I was forgetting something that would cost me: a bad grade, a black mark, or being disciplined for poor behavior. I was a sensitive kid, and I am now a sensitive adult. I wear my emotions on my sleeve, but few can discern what is unfolding behind the smile I wear. It is a purposefully placed mask meant to keep people at a distance. A smile signals to the world that everything is fine. In fact, a smile can be a protective shield; if people see a smile, they are less likely to begin asking probing questions.

Take a few minutes to consider and respond to these questions. Do you typically wear a mask during any part of your day? If so, what kind of mask do you most often wear? Why? What is the mask hiding? Make a list. We will examine your answers tomorrow.

DAY THREE

With your answers from yesterday's questions in hand, let's examine them. Although I, obviously, cannot see your responses, I would bet that they all tie into Fear in some way. You wear a mask so as not to be judged. You fear being misunderstood, or of being judged unfairly. You fear people knowing too much about you, revealing too much of you. You fear being found out, shamed, ostracized. Whatever your fear, look to the Word of God for the truth. Scripture teaches that God loves you unconditionally. Even though you may keep obsessive track of your every sin, failure, accident, and mistake, God sees you in a different light. If you have surrendered your life to Jesus, and He is your personal Lord and Savior, then you have been made righteous through Him. If you always have a running list of your setbacks in the back of your mind, take time to write them down. Do not rehearse the scenes so you relive them; just write down the scenarios. Get them on paper where you can see them. Do not drag yourself through the insult heap, or lambast yourself for the flubs and errors you have made. Instead, take your list and fold it in half.

In that blank space, write in big, bold print: **SHAME HAS NO HOLD ON ME**.

DAY FOUR

I was an anxious child, born into a family prone to worry and anxiety. However, after my stroke, I confronted new opponents, new levels of worries and concerns. I believe that regardless of the level of Anxiety you are grappling with, the same can be said of each. Fear's goal is to minimize the appearance of God while at the same time to elevate and inflate the fearful thoughts you have. In this paradigm God feels distant, and you feel abandoned and powerless to change the situation. In this context, fear becomes a choice. "Do not be afraid," and similar phrases occur numerous times in the Bible. It is what the angels said when they revealed themselves to the shepherds at the time of Jesus' birth. God said the same to Joshua: "Have I not commanded you? Be strong and courageous. Do not be afraid; do not be discouraged, for the Lord your God will be with you wherever you go" (Joshua 1:9). What do we gather from this verse? It is the Lord's presence that makes the difference. We can be strong, and we can be courageous. Why? Because He accompanies us. When we realize just how close He is to us, Fear cannot hold us back. We become encouraged. God is magnified, while Fear is dwarfed.

DAY FIVE

For today's meditation, allow me to share with you a poem I wrote entitled, "*One Lie.*" I suggest you read it slowly, thoughtfully, and reflectively. Tomorrow I will reveal the poem's origin as well as the Scripture that inspired it.

One Lie

An oppressive cloud hangs just over my head

it's out of sight, but its presence is felt,

making me apprehensive

I am tempted to become anxious, to become overwhelmed,

but I realize my God is present; He is right beside me,

So, I will not be shaken, I will not tremble, I will not grow fearful

I do not know what triggers this attack, welcomes this foreboding entity

because I do not enjoy its company;

I do not want it to remain with me

My mind wanders down a darkened path

troubling thoughts spring to life; they are not my own

the atmosphere is different ... unpleasant, uncomfortable

A lie I have resisted in blurting out is now front and center in my mind

I pull away from it, look for distractions, but there, the ugly idea stands

I am afraid that if I speak it, Evil will pounce upon it, give life to it,

and cause me to experience a deeper degree of despair

I know what is wrong ...

I have discerned the lie, but what to do?

to let the enemy know that I am bothered, that I am afraid of this thought?

to let him know that he has successfully penetrated my thoughts,

and now I am fixated on this one thing?

I am exasperated … distraught

but I am not alone in this struggle

Something within roars back,

resists buckling to the Fear surrounding me

in the midst of this, His Spirit speaks to me

My Rescuer makes His presence known

and I feel a sense of relief wash over me

my confidence is anchored in Him, not in my own strength or ability

His Word acts as a suit of armor for me

I am wrapped inside,

Well-protected, safe and secure

What I had read on days previously

what I had meditated on in the past came to the forefront of my mind,

crowding out the lie and the associated worries

I became transfixed on Jesus, and in that moment ...

I was released

free from the spell that seemed to bind me, that paralyzed me

and filled me with dread

The light came down and pierced the darkness that entrapped me

I was at peace ...

joy grew inside of me

hope entered my lungs and calmed my breathing

I rejoice now, in my Deliverer coming to me in my time of need

and delivering me from my enemy

He fights for me, He fights for you, relentlessly, with zeal

He is present, He is always right there, just within reach

He hears your faintest whisper and He responds,

Hallelujah!

DAY SIX

I wrote this poem on March 7, 2019, the six-year anniversary of my stroke. I had written it soon after experiencing an anxiety attack. Such attacks are infrequent, and I thank God for that because they are unpleasant and exhausting. You probably know exactly what I am talking about. I realize these attacks can be crippling to some. They can last a few minutes or go on for hours. The beginning of this poem is based on a verse I have recently come across that I have found to be critical in winning my fight against Anxiety. Simply dwell on this verse and, if possible, commit it to memory. If that is too challenging, write it down and display it somewhere where you can easily see it. Here it is:

> *"I know the Lord is always with me. I will not be shaken, for he is right beside me" (Psalm 16:8 NLT).*

The poem is rooted in this verse and the truth that it contains: God is with you. Where is He? Right beside you. This revelation transformed my encounters with Anxiety. I receive strength and vitality because I do not face Anxiety alone, but while standing beside the Creator and Sustainer of Life. Declare this word aloud. Whenever you face Anxiety and are tempted to fret, speak this verse aloud. Let it pierce the false notion that you are weak, that you are alone, that you are powerless. The words thrown at you are nothing more than lies, and you do not have to receive them. Overrule the lies and the disparaging thoughts with the Truth. Always interject the Word of God in your fights. It is our weapon.

DAY SEVEN

One verse that has also played a key role in my own fight is one that is probably quite familiar to you:

> *"For God has not given us a spirit of fear and timidity, but of power, love, and self-discipline"* (2 Timothy 1:7 NLT).

This is another verse worth committing to memory or keeping close by. Wielding the Word is not always an easy thing to do. Situations, circumstances, and events outside of our control can challenge us, challenge the Word. However, the Word ministers to us. In this instance, it reminds us of who we are. Despite our feeling fearful or timid, we see that this is not from God. We were not made to resemble such characteristics. Who are you? What has God given you? The answer is contained within this verse from 2 Timothy. You are a recipient of a spirit that embodies power, love, and self-discipline (or in some translations, a sound mind). Recite this verse, but make it personal, make it a personal declaration. Speak it often over yourself, allow His Word to transform your perception of yourself.

DAY EIGHT

Let us look at an example in the Book of Judges of a young man who had a choice to make: to continue to believe that he was weak, small, and therefore unusable by God, or to abandon those excuses and embrace the words the Lord had spoken concerning him. The story of Gideon is one of my favorites in the Bible. Gideon's situation is not so relatable, but his mindset certainly is. In Judges chapter six, Gideon has a conversation with the angel of the Lord, asking why God would abandon Israel, and give them to the Midianites. In verse 14 (NLT), "Then the angel turned to him and said, 'Go with the strength you have, and rescue Israel from the Midianites. I am sending you!'"

What is Gideon's response? He struggles with what he has been told to do. He confesses his doubts in verse 15 by saying, "But Lord…how can I rescue Israel? My clan is the weakest in the whole tribe of Manasseh, and I am the least in my entire family!" The chapter begins with Israel crying out to the Lord for deliverance from the Midianites. They acknowledge that there is an issue—they are oppressed—and they are seeking deliverance.

They are looking for a solution. Who should God send to act as a deliverer? A young man who thought so little of himself that he immediately assumed that the task assigned to him was too great for him to accomplish.

Even though Gideon felt completely inadequate for the mission, as if the Lord had given him this assignment by accident, God knew exactly who He was speaking to. How did He first address Gideon? "Mighty hero, the Lord is with you!" (v. 12b). God saw something in Gideon that he couldn't see in himself—the traits of a warrior. We see those traits play out over the next few chapters. Read the story for yourself. Take some time to read attentively Judges chapters 6-8. Notice the transformation Gideon undergoes: from a reserved, doubt-riddled young man to a conquering hero, who is even talked about by the enemy in their camps (Judges 7:13-14). The enemy knows him by name, and they interpret the dream as a foreshadowing of their defeat—which is exactly what happens. Gideon attacks with a mere 300 men, and the Lord routs the enemy, causing them to turn on each other and retreat in panic. Gideon pursues, and by the end of the fight has killed 120,000 Midianites and members of their allies. What made the difference? How could this young man be changed so drastically? Judges 6:14 provides the answer: the presence of the Lord was with Gideon.

DAY NINE

After his initial conversation with the Lord, Gideon requested a series of signs to confirm that this was in fact the Lord. What was God's response? Did He grow impatient or angry? Did He become disappointed with Gideon and his lack of confidence in the words spoken to him? No. He waited for Gideon to prepare Him a meal, then consumed it in fire while it sat on a rock. Later, Gideon asked for two additional signs: a fleece wet with dew while the surrounding ground was dry, and then a dry fleece while the surrounding ground was wet with dew. God delivered each sign Gideon asked for.

Why did Gideon test the Lord in such a way? Because he knew that apart from God he could not carry out the mission given to him. At first, he made excuses, likely linked to embedded insecurities and oft-rehearsed lies concerning himself. While Gideon saw himself as weak, insignificant, and incapable, God saw something else; Gideon's potential greatness, and reaffirmed His presence with him. With a God-given strategy Gideon and his 300 men, assisted later by Israelites from the tribes of Naphtali, Asher, and

Ephraim, routed and destroyed a 120,000-strong enemy army. As a result of Gideon's willingness to believe the words given to him by God, he played an instrumental role in releasing his people from the rule of the Midianites.

What problems, issues, injustices, or other evils do you see around you? What if God approached you and said He would use you as the solution? How would you respond? Like Gideon, by throwing out a series of excuses? If everyone else responded in the same way, would anything change? Your attitude might be, "How can I do this," when it should be, "Why can't I do this? Why can't God use me?" He uses imperfect people each and every day to advance His kingdom, to make His heart known. The Bible is filled with individuals who, once yielded to Him, humbly submitted to Him, and placed their trust in Him; did extraordinary feats. Words might be holding you back, or painful memories. You may be holding onto mislabels and misperceptions. Maybe you see yourself in a distorted light. To combat these negative and hurtful words you need to be aware of how God sees you right now. So, think back and glean from your past encouraging words, encounters that made you smile, that reaffirmed a dream or aspiration. What are titles you wear proudly? Has anyone ever given you a prophetic word or words? What does God say about you? Let us dive into that subject next.

DAY TEN

The Word of God holds a number of descriptors that apply to you. Despite what you might think about yourself, or the opinions of other people, will you allow His words to take refuge inside of you? Will you take time to meditate on them, to allow them to penetrate down into your heart, into your soul? Here are a few things God says about you, and I would encourage you to explore the Scriptures and discover for yourself exactly how God sees you. You could very well walk away from your search surprised and motivated to spur yourself onward.

- **Romans 8:37** says that we are "more than conquerors" in Christ.
- **Romans 8:14** reveals that because we have His Spirit living inside of us, we are children of God. We have been adopted into God's family through Christ and thus have the right and privilege to call God *Abba*, or Father. We are no

longer slaves to fear but redeemed and deeply loved children of God.

- **1 Peter 2:9** describes us as "a chosen people, a royal priesthood, a holy nation, God's special possession" in order that we might offer Him praise because He called us "out of darkness into his wonderful light."
- **Philippians 4:13** declares that we can "do everything through Christ, who gives [us] strength" (NLT). It is an oft quoted verse, but it is the truth; we can do everything God requires of us or allows us to go through because He equips us with His strength. Again, look at what Gideon accomplished. His encounter with God completely transformed him. The reason he accomplished so much is because he listened to and obeyed the Lord. He placed his fears, his doubts, and his insecurities on the shelf and decided to trust God, and to walk out the calling presented to him. His decision had a profound impact on the quality of life for a multitude. He liberated an entire people and brought down a mighty enemy.

Believe it or not, you are the answer to somebody's prayer. You possess traits and abilities to positively and dynamically change the world around you—with the Lord's help—should you choose to do so. Take time here to explore both the Old and New Testaments and discover for yourself at least three verses or passages that speak on your identity, who God fashioned you to be, who you are in Christ, and/or your purpose. I would suggest taking time to Google/research your name, find out its origin and its meaning. Let Christ be the foundation on which you build your life. Let His life-giving Word influence you, shape you and define you.

1. ____

2. ____

3. ____

DAY ELEVEN

Let us backtrack a bit. How would you define Anxiety? ______

____

____

____

____

____

Merriam-Webster defines anxiety as, "characterized by extreme uneasiness of mind or brooding fear about some contingency."

Anyone who struggles with Anxiety knows that worry remains a constant thought throughout the day, a nagging, persistent uneasiness that lingers. It is a powerful, foreboding feeling that often unnerves a person. Personally, whenever I suffer an anxiety attack, I feel like my mind is being invaded by a belligerent and unwelcome force. Just prior to the attack I usually feel uneasy;

something just seems "off," or out of alignment. Perhaps you can relate to this. I often feel as if something is creeping up on me, typically on my left side. I feel disconnected, as if someone has flipped a switch. I am aware of what is going on around me but feel like I am just part of the background scenery. My stomach churns to the point of making me feel nauseous. I feel unsteady on my feet, as though I need to sit down. I shut down, more or less. This sense of discombobulation can last minutes or hours, and often I am forced to think back over the course of the day or week in order to pinpoint the cause. It takes sifting—sometimes a lot—but eventually I figure it out. Small, seemingly innocent and harmless thoughts pass through our minds in the course of every day, and we usually think little about them, and don't need to. Sometimes, though, your subconscious grips one, and then another, and another, stresses over each one, and nurtures them until worry and Anxiety becomes the predominant feature on the landscape of your mind.

I have gotten into the practice, when going to bed, of laying down my anxious thoughts before falling asleep. I ask the Lord to alleviate any and all of my worries or fearful thoughts. 2 Corinthians 10:5 tells us that we have the ability to take every thought captive and make it obedient to Christ. So, when I become aware that my stream of thoughts is souring, or I am allowing worries to prevail, and the mindset of my "old man" attempts to assert itself and take control, I just tell myself that I am conforming my thoughts to God's thoughts, placing my fear-tinged ideas under the blood of Jesus. I take authority over my thoughts and am unwilling to give room in my mind to the enemy. I want to be so aware of God's presence that I am neither interested nor engaged in worrying, or in multiplying my worries. I remind myself that I am loved and adored by Father, and that nothing can separate me from that reality.

Read Romans 8:37-39. Let the truth sink deep into your spirit that there is *nothing* that can separate you from the love of God. He is pursuing you with an everlasting, unconditional love. He gives you grace for each day. Allow the glorious revelation contained in these verses to wash over you like a flood. Read it slowly, highlight it, circle it, write it down separately. Even taking a few minutes to meditate on it will do you good. Love drives out or casts out Fear. So, refresh yourself in the Truth, knowing that you are loved. Christ died for you so that you might experience a fully restored connection to Him. You have full access to the Father through Christ, and you can boldly approach His throne without reservation. So, whenever Fear tries to overwhelm you, declare loudly and with confidence, "I am a much-loved child of God! Nothing will be able to separate me from the love of God that is in Christ Jesus my Lord!"

DAY TWELVE

Let me introduce the beginning of a second poem I wrote, entitled, "We Venture Out."

Where is light needed?

In darkness …

As children of light, recipients of God's Holy Spirit

Where are we needed? Where do we need to go?

Into the Darkness …

Though we may be fearful, hesitant to enter the shadows

our great big, all powerful, all knowing God goes before us

what should we be afraid of?

The thought of light and the role it plays is what sparked the creation of this piece. Light invades the Darkness, and reveals what lies in the shadows. The idea of venturing into new territory, of facing personal demons, of confronting monsters, is an intimidating thought, but the truth is God is with us. If we look to Romans 8:31, we find this empowering truth: "If God is for us, who can be against us?" By following His promptings, by obeying His commands, and by serving Him whole-heartedly, we will find the grace and the strength to move forward, to endure. There will be opposition, of course, as the enemy does not want us to gain ground; he does not want us to reap the harvest. Oftentimes the presence of opposition is a sign that we are in fact moving in the right direction.

I mean, for example, the creation of this book has not necessarily been an easy project. I have had anxious thoughts during this preliminary stage. I have questioned my own qualifications for piecing together a devotional and wondered whether it flows together well enough or is just a disjointed mess. Yet, a number of people have told me that this would be beneficial to them. My mission in life is to encourage people, to inspire others, to see them be liberated from lies and living life fully engaged, investing their full potential, seeing dreams fully manifest. Doubts come and go, anxieties flicker. However, I am choosing to push ahead, to move forward with this project believing that my own testimony can impart courage and hope.

Sometimes all we have to do is persevere in light of what we might be seeing or experiencing. The daily decision to keep moving builds character, adds strength, and trains us as warriors for the fight. So, exercise regularly with the verses I am providing, and add more of your own. Getting the Word of God engrained in you will enable you to persevere, to fight through to triumph. This way you add more weapons to your arsenal, so to speak, and the Holy Spirit is present to teach, guide, and counsel you. He offers revelation when you are examining and meditating on the Word of God. (You may refer to Colossians 1:9-11 in regards to the Spirit as a teacher, or John 14:26. Additional verses may include Luke 12:12 and 1 John 2:27)

DAY THIRTEEN

Here is the second stanza of my poem, "We Venture Out":

If Heaven is spurring us onward, how can we do anything but be complicit?

If Heaven is cheering us on, how can we shrink back?

If our God is for us, who can possibly stand against us?

So, we can boldly enter the Darkness, expecting our God to fulfill His role

He pours Himself out, through us, and radiates outward

performing inexplicable feats, ministering to the crowds,

rendering impossibilities weak,

incapable of preventing His will from occurring

The idea is simple. God uses people to interject light, to be His hands and feet in the world, to bear influence in changing the culture, in bringing God to meet situations and circumstances. There is a need. We carry the solution. However, in administering the cure, we must acknowledge most assuredly that we will face resistance, even, sometimes, from those closest to us. God offers us vision, and sometimes we cannot successfully transfer that vision to others. We see possibility where others see only improbability or outright failure. Change comes at a cost, and positive change will be hindered by the powers of Darkness that will fight not to yield ground and lose souls in the process. The aim of our enemy is plainly and succinctly disclosed in John 10:10: "The thief comes only to steal, kill and destroy; I have come that they may have life, and have it to the full." Whether we realize it or not, we are engaged in a war. We are participants in a global spiritual conflict that, thankfully, is already decided.

We fight from a victor's stance because Jesus has already overcome. He defeated hell and broke the curse of Sin and Shame, liberating us from the Darkness by paying a debt too great for us to repay. It is important for you to realize that to whatever degree you are battling Anxiety, there is a spiritual component to it. You will not experience lasting peace until you spend time in the Lord's presence, in prayer, not just sharing your heart, but also listening to Him. You can pray for deliverance from Fear, receive the impartation of courage, you can be inspired to act courageously, but until you understand who you are in Christ, and believe that you are loved, that you are a fearsome warrior in Christ, that in His hands you are a force to be reckoned with, the doubts will ruminate, confidence will prove elusive, and you will be thrown about constantly by the opinions of others. This has to be a settled issue inside of you. It is your choice and your choice alone to make.

When feelings of Anxiety begin to stir, and you find your thoughts being overcrowded by worries, learn to stand up tall and say, "I was made for this! I AM a victor in Christ! I AM NOT a victim! I AM NOT powerless! I believe in my God, and in the greatness of my God! I am redeemed. I am a restored soul, imperfect, but an effective instrument. Darkness … Fear … you have no hold on me. I curse the chains that are attempting to bind me, silence me, immobilize me. In Jesus' name, I cancel the assignment of the enemy. Father, remind me in this moment how much You love me, and that nothing can separate me from it. Remind me that there is a sufficient amount of grace for every day, and that I am not striving to win Your affection or approval. I am covered by the blood of Jesus. I am an overcomer. I can do all things through Christ who strengthens me, who fuels me, who moves me. I am not weak. I am not so fractured that I am unusable, incapable of impacting a region or the generations. You have something good for me. I will not surrender my hope, my joy, or my peace. I will not stop pressing in, pushing ahead. Fear, you are in my way. Move, or be run over, because, I am not relenting! You will not prevent me from fulfilling my mission. You will not keep me from my promised land. God is with me, so I will keep advancing. My eyes are fixed on Him, and that is all that matters. Thank You, Lord! In Jesus' name I pray, Amen."

DAY FOURTEEN

How do you divide your time on a typical day? How do you spend your free time? What do you often listen to? What kind of people do you spend time with? Who is in your close-knit circle? Many things, many voices, try to influence us every day. Some are positive, encouraging streams vying for your attention. Others are negative, condescending, and disparaging forces at play, undermining your efforts, discouraging you from pursuing a dream or becoming anything more than what you are currently. We absorb whatever surrounds us, especially if that is a habitual environment for us. If we want to maintain hope, we have to find sources that espouse hopefulness and allow them to inundate our hearts and minds. What kind of language do you most often hear? Does it build up, or tear down? Do you hear that language coming from your own mouth?

I recall being in a group of people, perhaps in a waiting room or somewhere similar, where, as often happens, someone in the group recognized another and began engaging in small talk, catching up with each other's lives. Their conversation soon transitioned from a friendly chat to a competition of sorts as to who had the more difficult life. If one complained of a problem, the other responded with an even worse situation. It seemed to me as though they were trying to outdo one another for the gain of some imaginary crown that would signify them as the most miserable in the room.

On another occasion, during my rehabilitation at the rehab hospital in Hershey, I remember a patient who was assigned to the room next to mine, who resisted performing the exercises prescribed to him by the therapists. Now, why would he do such a thing? I think it was, in part, because he lacked hope. He was an older man, probably sixty-plus, who lacked the support network that I had. I received visitors and had mail arriving daily. Words of encouragement were spoken to me every day. I was looking ahead with expectation of being released from the hospital and moving on with life. I'm not sure what he had lying ahead of him, if anything. He had no motivation to get better, and so he quit. I wonder what happened to him, and where he is now. I wonder about the other people I met during my hospitalization, the other patients, whether or not they are enjoying a high-quality life.

I can understand how easily someone who has had their health and wellbeing jeopardized can sink into a depression. The fear you face in a near-death scenario is jarring; an internal switch is flipped, and you are left to contemplate life and all of its intricacies. You reprioritize. You reconfigure how you allot your time, and make an effort to better yourself in body, mind, and soul. While a patient in the hospital, I often wondered about my own recovery, how I would recover, or even whether I would recover. My body was broken, and my mind left in a damaged state. I was concerned, unsure of how I would move forward. My plans, my goals, everything I was striving to accomplish—all of that was put on hold. My life was interrupted. All I could do was stand there in a daze and watch the world turn, watch events unfold, watch as my friends made progress in establishing lives of their own. I was forced to sit out, for a time, and I believe that time has now passed. But there was a season where my future seemed unsure. I could have feared the uncertainty about tomorrow, and I did—and sometimes still do. Life's unpredictable nature often is a frightening prospect. Today, everything is moving along as expected, pleasantly, happily, and then, in the blink of an eye, it is lost in smoke and flame.

Every day I am met by some form of encouragement. I receive a word from someone, read a post on my Facebook or via Instagram. I listen to a lot of music that reinforces my faith and helps me keep my focus on God. I turn to worship music, especially songs of praise. What we listen to influences our thoughts, and our thoughts have a profound and lasting impact on our attitudes, on our words, and on our actions. I left the hospital expecting to regain abilities lost to me, to regain a sense of independency, to regain myself, but without encouragement, without those various streams of encouragement flowing into me, I would have left Hershey broken, bitter, and brooding over what was lost, what was wrong, unable to think beyond my physical limitations. I would have soured, and most likely self-destructed. I would have quit.

Here are a few songs that have encouraged me and continue to do so. They address Fear and put it in its proper place, in its proper context. I will provide the titles; you seek out the lyrics. Turn to YouTube or Google. Listen to each one and listen to this collection often to build yourself up. Use them as personal declarations over yourself. Use them as weapons against the enemy, against the Anxiety you are facing, and watch the monster shrink. Find other songs, other encouraging, soul-lifting resources that will feed you with good, reaffirming words. Shift your focus away from Fear and onto God. Magnify His name, give Him praise, elevate His name, and you will see your lens change, your reality take on a different light. You will see your circumstances, your situations, your problems, and your worries differently.

- "No Longer Slaves" by Melissa and Jonathan Helser
- "Raise A Hallelujah" by Bethel Music
- "Holy Ground" by Melodie Malone
- "Because He Lives" by Bill Gaither and the Gaither Vocal Band
- "Stand in Your Love" by Josh Baldwin

DAY FIFTEEN

In Numbers chapter 13, God instructs Moses to send out twelve men to scout out the land of Canaan, the land promised to the Israelites. Each of the twelve tribes are represented by one leader. After receiving specific instructions from Moses, the men set out and explored the land for forty days, gathering some of its fruit and observing the communities of those peoples already occupying the land. In Numbers 13:26 the scouts return to the Israelite camp and make their report to Moses and Aaron, and all the people. While all twelve agree that the land is good, flowing in milk and honey, they differ in their opinion concerning whether or not the Canaanites can be conquered. They note that some of the occupants are giants, and that the cities are large and well-fortified. They describe the people of the land as powerful. All but two of the spies insist on the futility of warring against these people; to them, taking the land is impossible. The two who believe otherwise are Caleb and Joshua. In verse 30, Caleb silences the people and encourages them to press forward to claim the land God has promised to them.

All of the scouts saw the same thing, the reality of the situation; why, then, did Caleb and Joshua react the way they did? Why did they disagree with the majority? What did Caleb and Joshua see differently? Verse 33 sheds some light on the discrepancy. The majority of the scouts revealed that in their own eyes they seemed like nothing more than grasshoppers, and that these foreigners, these giants would see them the same way. Their self-perception was lacking; they viewed themselves as small, feeble, and weak, wholly incapable of warring successfully against the occupants and taking the land. In Numbers 14:6-9, Caleb and Joshua make an impassioned plea to the nation to remain faithful to God and not to fear the supposed obstacles. Specifically, in verse 9, they say to the people, "Only do not rebel against the Lord. And do not be afraid of the people of the land, because we will devour them. Their protection is gone, but the Lord is with us. Do not be afraid of them." Caleb and Joshua, unlike the majority of their scouting companions, were aware that God was for them, that He was with them. That simple truth made all the difference. Hope of taking the land remained possible in their minds because of God's presence. They saw the same issues, the same challenges, but instead of becoming fearful they rose up in faith and said, "we can overcome because God is for us."

How do you view yourself? In the space below write down several adjectives that you think accurately describe you.

____

____

____

Do you have a dream or a goal that has not yet fully manifested? Does it often seem just out of reach? What is stopping you from obtaining it? What giants stand in your way? Take time to reflect. Consider what you would like to accomplish and what prevents you from doing it. Then add the phrase, "but God is with me." Ask Him for wisdom, for insight as to what you can do in this moment to move one step closer to obtaining that dream. In this moment you have more than you know at your disposal. You have a mighty, uncontestable God at your side, and He will reveal Himself in your pursuit of your promised land. Just choose to keep your eyes on Him. The problems, the hindrances, the impediments are real, but they do not have to permanently bar you from entering and claiming what is yours.

DAY SIXTEEN

How did the people respond to Joshua and Caleb? Not as you might imagine. Their response was rooted in Fear. Instead of being encouraged by what Caleb and Joshua said, instead of looking to God, they chose to threaten the lives of both men: "But the whole assembly talked about stoning them" (Numbers 14:10). Speaking the Truth is not always received warmly. The Israelites as a whole perceived themselves as weak, as incapable of taking the land, and in their minds erroneously shrank God to fit those preconceived notions. How did God respond to this blatant rejection? "The Lord said to Moses, 'How long will these people treat me with contempt? How long will they refuse to believe in me, in spite of all the signs I have performed among them?'" God then declared his intention to destroy the people, but Moses intervened on their behalf. Instead of destroying the people outright, God directed them into the wilderness. This portion of the journey was intended to remove the grumblers and complainers, those critical of the Lord who chose not to believe but to disobey. An entire generation was set to expire in the wilderness before the Lord would bring the people into the promised land.

Consider those things that make you afraid. Make a list, either on paper or in your mind. What concerns you, what causes you to worry unceasingly? Beside each of those points write or shout out loud, "My God is bigger!" Remind yourself of those times where He delivered you, where He did a miracle, where He gave you an answer. Let those memories bolster your faith.

When the enemy has come at me with different threats, causing me to wonder if I will soon perish, I just recount the fact that God preserved my life in March of 2013. When the enemy attacks me, one of his preferred tactics is to plant in my head the thought that if I do this or that, I risk my life. He attacks me most often while I am involved in my everyday tasks. Nighttime especially can be a jostling, unnerving time of day. I have woken up at times wondering whether I was experiencing another stroke. I have left my tablet or phone by my bed more times than I care to admit, just as a precaution, in case something would happen. But in the midst of these battles I remind myself that God has my story mapped out from beginning to end. He didn't save me just to let me go now. I refute the devil's claims with what I know to be true, with what I have experienced. He cannot win against me when I have decided that God trumps my fears. I am not going to cause myself to become panic-stricken because I have chosen to focus on the wrong thing, to empower the Fear. I choose to disarm it by declaring in the moment that my God is able to deliver me and has a hope and a future plan for my life. We must get into the habit of striking back against the Fear. We do not have to just sit and wallow in it, allowing it to become bigger and more intimidating. We can speak against it. We must refute it, argue against it, be mindful that we can fight back, that we can hit it hard and undermine its points. We must take hold of the initiative and not lose it.

DAY SEVENTEEN

Consider the story of David and Goliath. It is a familiar story, one taught to most of us at an early age. Some of us might recall our Sunday school teacher retelling the story by using felt cutouts on a decorated board. If you need to refresh yourself with the details of the story, turn to 1 Samuel 17. To summarize, the Israelites and the Philistines faced off against each other across a valley. Goliath, a giant, was the champion of the Philistine army. He was an impressive figure whose presence terrified the Israelite army and King Saul. Every day for 40 days, Goliath, with extreme arrogance, leveled taunts against the Israelites. He challenged them to send their own champion against him in one-to-one combat. The losers would become slaves of the victors. Not one soldier in Israel's army accepted Goliath's challenge. This giant was, in a way, Fear personified.

After 40 days of Goliath's belittling taunts toward the Israelites, David arrived on the scene. He was delivering some foodstuffs to his three oldest brothers who were serving in Saul's army. David saw Goliath and heard his taunts, and he responded with courage.

He sought to accept the challenge and believed himself capable of defeating the giant. What made this small, young shepherd boy think he could accomplish this seemingly impossible task? His past experience. His discovery of God's faithfulness. King Saul protested that David, of all the men present, should be the one to face Goliath. David's reply to the king reveals how this small shepherd viewed God. He explained to the king how in the past he had fought lions and bears with a club. Whenever one of these beasts came to steal away or threaten one of his lambs, he pursued it and killed it. In each of those instances God had protected him and enabled him to protect his flock.

David was insulted that this Philistine was permitted to speak about the God of Israel in such a degrading fashion with complete impunity. He recognized that this giant had insulted the honor of God and he wanted to rectify it. In verse 26, David asks the soldiers around him, "Who is this pagan Philistine that he should defy the armies of the living God?" He sees the same reality as the soldiers around him, but unlike them, he sees the giant in context. He sees him as an impediment, an obstacle that God will assist him in bringing down.

The king gives him armor to wear and a sword to wield, but the equipment is too large, heavy, and bulky for David to wear. So, he goes into battle with a sling, his shepherd's staff, and five smooth stones picked up from a streambed. To anyone there, David must have appeared wholly unprepared for the fight and would be easily overmatched by the battle-hardened giant. David and Goliath exchanged words as they closed the distance between them. David's final words before the confrontation, recorded in verses 45-47, declare his confidence that the Lord will give Goliath over to him, and that the giant will fall. With Goliath's defeat, "the whole world will know that there is a God in Israel" (1 Sam. 17:46c).

David had confidence in God. His past battles and previous triumphs had prepared him for this moment, and against all human odds, he killed Goliath, cut off his head, and thereby caused the Philistine army to rout. You do not have to allow Fear to taunt you, to confine you, to fill you with dread without consequences. You have a voice, you possess the Word of God, you have been given His Holy Spirit. Be like David in the sense of talking back to the Fear that you face. Remember where God has brought you from, and what He has led you through. Take courage, for God is with you and He will guide your hands in toppling the giants that oppose you. Let your faith speak; let it shout, let it defy the enemy.

DAY EIGHTEEN

One way to shift your focus from Fear to God is to partake of communion. Normally, communion is taken in the communal setting of a worship service, but I believe you can take part in this meal of remembrance alone. Jesus broke bread and drank wine for the Passover meal with His disciples before his trial, death, and resurrection. For us, this has become the Lord's Supper. We break bread and drink wine or grape juice so that we might remember the sacrifice Jesus made on our behalf. The bread represents His body, and the wine symbolizes His blood. His body was broken for us, and His blood shed to atone for our sins. Isaiah 53 is a prophetic revelation concerning Jesus and what His sacrifice provides for us. We break the bread and drink from the cup in memory of Him, to honor Him. It is an act that is often and appropriately accompanied by reflection. It is an act of reverence. Jesus took upon Himself our weaknesses, our sorrows, our rebellion, our sins, our sicknesses, and our diseases. Jesus sacrificed Himself so that we could be made whole, restored, and healed. He broke the curse of Sin and buried Shame. The love of God was greater, and He sought to rescue us from an eternity spent apart from Him.

By taking communion, you can shift your focus, reaffirming the Truth that Jesus died for you. He thought you valuable, He thought you worthy. The cross stands as a testament of God's love. John 3:16-17 says, "For God so loved the world that he gave his one and only Son, that whoever believes in him will not perish but have eternal life. For God did not send his Son into the world to condemn the world, but to save the world through him." God wants to see you fully restored, made whole. He does not want to see you cowering, living life as anything less than His son or daughter, His beloved child. He does not want to watch you capitulate on any of the rich blessings He has for you so that you might gain a shaky agreement with Fear. Fear wants to rule your life, to exert cruel dominion over you. By taking communion you are reaffirming that Jesus Christ is your personal Lord and Savior, and it is a declaration professing that His sacrifice brings healing and restoration to every part of your life. So, gather the necessary elements and partake of the Lord's Supper, or gather a small group and have a time of fellowship. Look to any of the Gospels and recount what Jesus said of the bread and the wine. Read Isaiah 53 to remind yourself of what Jesus accomplished on the cross for you. Make this personal. He died for you because He loves you. That is what the cross says—I did this for you.

DAY NINETEEN

Many of my anxious thoughts have been about my health. When your health is broken, you re-prioritize things around you. Your outlook on life is different. Fear has preyed upon me, seeking out vulnerable moments where it can tear into me, and cause me a terrific amount of distress. On August 11, 2019, I stepped out in faith, responding to a conviction I felt regarding being baptized. A few years ago, I had been baptized; I have a certificate to prove it. However, after hearing a message given by Pastor Dave Hess on the subject of baptism and hearing the heart's cry of Pastor Eric Nehrt to see people released and unburdened through the act of baptism, I felt convicted. I felt the need to re-enter the water. I wanted to bury the old man, the old nature, habits, and mindsets I had become dependent on. I wanted to bury my anxious tendencies and be released from the bondages that held me to Fear. I was one of over 160 people to be baptized that day. Many of us had signed up and gone through a class on baptism, but a number of others, moved by the display, decided spontaneously to join the ranks of the baptized.

One bit of homework we were asked to complete prior to being baptized was a prophetic act. We were to write down a series of things: the names of people that had hurt us; people we needed to forgive; thoughts, mindsets, and lies that we knew were not of God; any works of the enemy; issues of the heart like bitterness, hatred, anger, or fear; sin issues, secret sins, habitual sins; need for physical healing. We were to take time to reflect, and to ask the Holy Spirit to give us insight into these matters and then write down anything that we felt fell under one of these categories. Each of us carried these lists into the water with us as an act of letting the old be put to death and buried. Upon emerging from the water, we were to take those soaked notes and throw them in the garbage, signifying the disconnect between the old self that entered the water, and the new self that emerged from the water. I believe things were left at the bottom of that tank, and I am free to let go of things, to not give in to temptation. I am not obligated to return to old, broken mindsets, nor to practice empty habits that have only served as coping mechanisms. I let go of Fear, of Bitterness, of Lust, of Envy when I went under the water that day. I also buried Shame.

Like any man, I have had my struggles with lust, and because of it I have been yoked to a fractured image of myself. I find myself now at 32 and never having engaged in a serious relationship. I sometimes grow anxious at the thought of living life alone, facing an unknown future without the support of a significant other. I am content living on my own, but I sometimes wonder if something is wrong with me, or if I just lack a certain trait that a woman is looking for in a guy. Lust has filled me with unrealistic expectations concerning relationships. My stroke only added to the number of my insecurities. Turning to lust can be described as a method of escape. I suppose a lot of guys become slaves to lust because it provides a means of getting away from reality. If you ask any guy about whether or not he has struggled with this at some time or other, almost every single one of them will answer yes. I may never meet a woman who I will fall in love with and call my wife; I know that is a possibility.

I now realize that life does not always resemble the picture you have in your head. Am I happy? Yes. However, I do realize there are better days ahead, and I am in a better position today than prior to being baptized. For me, and I believe for others, Shame and Fear are linked; they feed one another, and as a result you feel less than, completely undeserving of God's unconditional love. The Truth remains though, despite the feeling, that as distant as you might feel from God, He is still capable of reaching you. There is no pit deep enough that the grace of God cannot find you and deliver you from whatever mess you may be in.

So, ask the Holy Spirit to reveal to you things from your past that are holding you in check. Make out a list like the one I created for my baptism. Are you toting around Shame? If so, you can be released from it today. Have you ever been baptized? If not, that might be key in gaining victory over Fear, burying it, and rendering it a powerless force in your life. Ask God to give you wisdom and discernment concerning whether or not the time is right to be baptized. That act could very well be the first step on the road that leads you away from Anxiety and brings you to a newly found confidence in Him. You will no longer be haunted by your past. You will see how He brought you through it all, up to this moment. He will redefine it. Your old nature will be put to death, and you will be raised up to new life in Christ. What a glorious beginning!

DAY TWENTY

Mark 5:25 tells us about a woman who suffered from a condition that caused her constant bleeding, which she had endured for twelve years. She had sought out doctor after doctor, hoping that one of them would be able to cure her, but her condition had proved to be untreatable. And to top it all off, her condition had worsened over the years and she was now penniless, having spent all her wealth on all those physicians who had been unable to do anything for her. In Jewish culture, according to Mosaic Law, a woman experiencing bleeding was considered unclean and therefore untouchable. So, imagine being in this woman's position. She has endured being ostracized from her community for twelve years. She has sought out medical professionals who were unable to help her. Her wealth is gone. Her health is deteriorating. Can you sense her desperation? Verse 26 reveals that she had heard about Jesus, about His miracles and the healings he had performed. She thought she could be healed by him, if she could just touch his robe (v. 28).

When she touched His garment, she was immediately healed; the bleeding stopped. In the same moment, Jesus detected that healing power had gone out from Him. He wanted to know who had touched Him, a seemingly impossible question to answer considering the crowd of people pressing in around him. But He looked around until His eyes fell upon her. Verse 33 shows us a frightened woman who is trembling on account of what she has just experienced. Jesus' response to her? "Daughter, your faith has healed you. Go in peace and be freed from your suffering" (v. 34).

This woman most likely bore a tremendous degree of shame as a result of her situation. She would have been treated as "less than" on account of something that she could not control. She had a choice to make, and she chose to step out in faith to receive healing from Jesus. I imagine that the thought crossed her mind, if even for a fraction of a second, "What if nothing happens?" However, Fear did not prevent her from trying, from taking a chance, and her risk paid off. She was immediately healed.

I believe that God can heal immediately. I also believe that healing often comes through a process. For me personally, I am walking through a healing process. Not only am I being healed in a physical sense, but also in emotional, psychological, and spiritual senses. I also believe that God uses medical professionals to administer healing. People are gifted as caregivers. They have an interest in healing persons, in discovering cures, in treating ailments, and in improving the health of men and women. There certainly is no shame in consulting physicians, specialists, psychologists, counselors, or therapists because these people can be instrumental in restoring broken bodies and broken souls. These people are trained to determine sicknesses, underlying issues afflicting a person, and what treatments are available to provide relief and healing. If you are experiencing something that you believe is negatively impacting you in some way, you should pray about it. Take it to God, but you may also want to consult with a medical or health expert, someone who will walk beside you, who will improve your present condition so that you might live the best possible life.

DAY TWENTY-ONE

While many of my anxious thoughts are connected to my health, many others are attached to my financial wellbeing. Many people, yourself included, perhaps, are troubled by their financial situation. I am a part-time deli-clerk. I like what I do, and it pays beyond the minimum wage, but I do not have stacks of cash laying around. I do not have a lot of extra in my bank accounts. To be honest, my savings account was hit pretty hard by my choice to pursue a master's degree. I thought the degree would help open doors to me, but so far that has not happened. I have had several opportunities, but one by one those doors closed.

A few years ago, I got myself into a serious bind by accumulating several thousand dollars' worth of credit card debt. I thought erroneously that by having three or four cards I could spread out my expenses and pay off each one in time. However, I never seemed to hit the principal thanks to the high interest rates. The bills added up to a sum that caused me great distress. My stress must have showed on my face and in my behavior, because not long after I realized my precarious position, my mom asked me what was wrong. I explained it all to her. My parents decided to help me out, and because of them I was freed from this huge burden. In the aftermath I decided that I needed to streamline the amount of credit cards I had in my wallet. I broke ties with all companies but one. It is good to show yourself capable of handling the responsibility of operating a credit card, but living on credit, or allowing those companies to essentially own you, is absolutely nerve-wracking.

I am not good when it comes to keeping track of my money, or in creating a budget. I have overdrawn from my checking account one time, and that was both embarrassing and horrifying. I know I need to reform my ways and do a better job with saving and setting aside something so I can invest in my future. I have room to grow in the world of personal finances, but I am not destitute. I live comfortably, and that is my goal. I do not wish to live extravagantly. I am trying to live within my means. Splurging for me is buying a few dollars' worth of trinkets at a local flea market or buying a new book. I am a simple guy with simple tastes.

If you struggle with personal finances, you would be wise to seek out resources provided by the likes of Dave Ramsey, or a ministry like Crown Financial Ministries. There are resources available to help, including apps that can help you budget and stay on track. Your bank might even offer services that can help you stay in the green and confident that you are being a good steward of your money. You do not have to lose sleep over the state of your finances, but more than likely you will have to make sacrifices and keep better track of where your money is going. Seek out some assistance, listen to the advice given you, and apply it. Watch things change for the better and see a new sense of peace overtake you.

DAY TWENTY-TWO

As I write this, it is August 16, 2019. Last evening, I had an unexpected encounter that I am still trying to process. On Wednesday, my mom flew out to visit my sister and brother-in-law in Idaho. In light of her absence, my grandmother, Nanni, sought to take me and my dad out to supper. My Aunt Dotti, and a family friend, Ginny, were to meet us at a restaurant in town at 6:30 p.m. When I arrived at the restaurant, the parking lot was packed. I opted to park in the adjoining lot of a business that had closed at 5 p.m. I decided to back in to make it easier to leave. My tires were almost up against the concrete parking curb. I hopped out and saw that my grandmother was already inside.

As I went inside, I passed a high-school classmate and friend of mine named Sean. We chit-chatted a bit and he asked if I happened to have any copies of my books with me. I told him yes, they were in my van. As we walked out to my van, we passed Aunt Dotti and Ginny. I told them I would be right back; I had a book sale to make. I knew I would have to pull the van up a bit to open the back hatch to access the books. No problem. He wanted a copy of each book (three poetry books and *Life Interrupted*). I signed each one for him, and he paid me. I needed to close the hatch, and I knew the parking curb was right there.

However, to get a better angle on closing the hatch, I attempted to step over the curb. Well, that did not prove successful. I can only guess, as it happened so quickly, that my left foot got hung up on the curb. My momentum carried me, and I ended up falling backwards, scraping my elbow and bumping the back of my head against the concrete exterior of the building. I was in disbelief as I sat there. I am always so careful about my head, and hitting it, even tapping it on something has been a deeply seated fear of mine. I didn't know how to react. I wanted to get up, but Sean told me to stay put. The whole thing happened right in front of him. He asked me what he should do. He suggested going into the restaurant to get my dad, who had arrived about the same time as Aunt Dotti and Ginny. I told him that would be best.

As I waited, I wondered whether I was about to take an ambulance ride, or would need to go back to Hershey, or have a CAT scan done. Then, out of the corner of my eye, I saw Dad walking towards me. He asked me if I was alright. I got back on my feet. There was a swollen knot on the back of my head, near the base of my skull, as wide as three fingers positioned side by side. My elbow looked the worst; it was scraped up pretty good and was bleeding. My right knee also had a minor scratch.

In short, our dinner plans were scrapped. Dad took me back to the house to clean up my wounds. He did his best and asked me if I wanted to stay at the house for the night. I agreed because I wasn't sure how badly I had hurt myself. Other than some anxious thoughts that had begun to stir, I felt fine, overall. Aunt Dotti offered to bring meals back to the house for us. Once I was bandaged up, Dad called Mom in Idaho. She was in shock, of sorts, kind of panicky, which is entirely understandable considering everything I have had to go through over the past six years. My sister, Hannah, got Mom calmed down. Hannah is currently working on a master's degree in speech pathology, so she knows anatomy and the human body. Mom wanted me to consult with somebody but didn't know who to refer me to. Urgent Care? No. ER? Maybe. Hershey? Maybe not. Then she mentioned contacting my chiropractor, Dr. Adam Keeler. He knows my history. He would be a good source to contact, so I sent him a message through Facebook. He responded quickly. He asked me the same questions my sister had already asked. He instructed us to ice the swelling, which we were doing, and to monitor my situation. If I began to vomit or experience cognitive issues, then I should proceed to the ER. I still felt fine. When talking with my Mom, she commented on how calm I sounded. She knows how I operate. I think hearing me helped ease her mind. Dad and I went to my apartment so I could grab pajamas, my toothbrush, and a massage wand because I knew I would be feeling the effects of that fall as the night wore on. We finally ate a little dinner at 9 p.m. After eating, I opted to lie in bed, while Dad chose to sleep in the recliner in the living room. He said he would check on me in the middle of the night. I brushed my teeth and then hit the hay. I slept pretty well, except for the blankets pulling at the bandage on my elbow.

I seem to be in good shape this morning. The elbow is healing, the knot on my head has gone down, and I am experiencing no issues with my vision, balance or coordination. So, Hannah, Mom, and I are all of the opinion that this accident happened so that I could see that I am tougher than I thought. On many days, I see myself as fragile and weak, not consciously, but definitely subconsciously. I have tried to stay within the confines of a bubble, not wanting to exert myself too much, trying not to fall, or trip, or bump into something. I am not a clumsy guy, but it is difficult to avoid every little mishap. My anxious thoughts have been geared towards a lot of "what if?" type scenarios, and I can easily get myself worked up. I always thought the worst would happen if I were to just bump my head against something, but now I find myself on this side of an accident still breathing, thinking, functioning, and just being me. An accident was bound to happen at some point. I could never keep myself accident-free 100% of the time. People trip and fall and have accidents every day; it is not an uncommon thing. I am not looking to experience more. I am not reckless. I continue to be cautious, but now I know that if something happens, it is not the end of the world.

Fear has not been an active force regarding this, not as much as what I initially thought. Today has been more emotional, though. I suppose the initial shock has now worn off. I have been praying and thanking God that it was not a worse accident. If I had hit the front of my head, I probably would have chosen a different course, but I believe I am alright. I am stronger than I thought, more resilient, and in better shape. I did read through Psalm 91, and I think you should do the same right now, as it is one that reminds the reader what degree of heavenly protection is offered to us as followers of Christ. It is an encouraging passage.

DAY TWENTY-THREE

Let us take a practical step in reducing anxious thoughts. Social media is a wonderful way to stay connected with friends and family members and to keep up to date on what is happening, but it is also a major throughway for negativity to seep into your personal space. Negative headlines are posted and reposted from the same outlets hourly. You can be inundated by messages requesting prayer for this or that. The world can appear to be falling apart. You can scroll through whole comment sections and be repulsed by the comments left behind. People are more apt to engage in bullying tactics when seated at home cloaked in anonymity as opposed to face-to-face confrontations. I have come across a host of ugly comments that reveal hatred contained within the heart. Enough time spent in this world can give you the impression that kindness is a relic of the past. This is, of course, not true, but there are people who become gleeful by tearing down others. They let loose a stream of disparaging words and systematically dismantle users just for kicks. Miserable people are set to make others miserable. Hurt people hurt others. Unhappiness and discontentment can be felt when reading many of these remarks.

If you are connected to social media sites like Facebook, Instagram, or Twitter, take time to examine the content. Make a note of how long you are on these platforms. Restrict yourself if need be so that you are not overwhelmed with the notion that the world is growing uglier. Every wave of violence is reported, personal needs are plastered all about, and it can quickly become too much to process. I know for myself that I just have to step away at times. I can feel the negativity clinging to me, the hopelessness beginning to establish roots inside of me. When I begin to feel that impulse, I know I need to step away. I do what I can in promoting positive stories. I share photographs I have taken, poems I have written, or entertaining stories I come across.

These platforms possess the potential to do a lot of good in bringing attention to some wonderful causes, and in keeping loved ones up to date with events and happenings, but it is vital that we are mindful of what passes through our ears and eyes. We need to be sure that we are devoting just as much, if not more, time connecting with God. We need to engage in conversations with Him, read His Word, and just be mindful of Him. Keeping our focus on Him keeps us refreshed and well-grounded. Daily encounters with Him preserve our hope, our joy, and our peace, and help us see people in the same light as He sees them. So, step away from social media if you need to; reduce the hours you spend on these sites. Be courteous, be respectful of others, and in a sea of negativity, offer your friends and followers something different. We are to be salt and light, and we can exemplify that through what we post, what we share, and what we leave for others to find.

It may be necessary to remove some persons from your sphere. You can unfollow certain ones, leave groups, mute conversations. You hold a lot of control over who enters your inner sphere, what comes into your world. Exercise that control by doing what is best for you, healthiest for your mindset. Guard the portals that allow Anxiety to access your mind and your soul and disconnect yourself from sources of unnecessary stress.

DAY TWENTY-FOUR

Philippians 4:6-7 is a familiar passage to many that is often quoted, and perhaps may prove to be a piece of your armor for combatting Anxiety. This is how the passage reads in the New Living Translation: "Don't worry about anything; instead, pray about everything. Tell God what you need and thank him for all he has done. Then you will experience God's peace, which exceeds anything we can understand. His peace will guard your hearts and minds as you live in Christ Jesus."

So, take time to consider this: How is your prayer life? How often do you pray? How often do you worry? I will be honest; I tend to worry more than I pray. I tend to worry first and pray later. Prayer should be a first response, a natural reaction to a need. Our minds can get in the way very quickly. I know for me that my mind often flies off the handle, and my imagination becomes engrossed in developing off-the-wall scenarios that just cause me more grief and adds fuel to the fire. I become anxious about things transpiring in a world of fantasy. They are intangible, but in my mind, they are playing out as if they are real. I feel, on the one hand, like I am doing myself a service by preparing myself for any possible situation, eliminating the unpleasant possibility of being surprised. On the other hand, however, I become paranoid, caught up in a state of panic. I simply become overwhelmed and unable to process what is happening. The answer for me, and for you, is simple – worry less and pray more. It sounds simple, and it is, but it is not an easy mode to transition into, especially if you tend to be a worrier by nature.

But, praise God, that old nature can be put to death. Tendencies, habits, mindsets, and patterns of thought must bow to the name of Jesus. In Him, we are new creations; our minds undergo a process of renewal. In Philippians 4:8, right after Paul encourages us to pray and ask God for what we need, he instructs us regarding what to focus our thoughts on. We are to fix our thoughts on what? Look up this verse and respond below.

What is ____________, ______________________, ____________, ____________, __________________, ______________________.

So, let us put this into practice. Write your top five worries. What is stressing you out right now?

____

____

____

____

____

____

Write them down, look at them, and instead of worrying about them any longer, pray about each. God already knows what is troubling you. Engage in a dialogue with Him. Ask Him how to handle each. Get into His Word; ask His Spirit to guide you through the books of the Bible. Use Google to your advantage. It is time to equip yourself, to find the tools that are at your disposal, and unleash them against the devil and hell's aim. If you forget what the enemy's intention is, look to John 10:10. It is time you stopped fighting the battles on your own and invite God to intercede on your behalf. Cease your worrying and give it to God. If you feel the need to worry, rise up, remind yourself that you gave it to God. Ask Him for what you need *and* thank Him for what He has already done.

Thankfulness is a powerful weapon. Counting your blessings, remembering what God has already done for you, and acknowledging His goodness and faithfulness extended to you revives hope inside of you. It rebukes despair, gloom, and bleakness. Down below, recount to yourself how God has proven Himself good and faithful to you. Count the blessings you have been given. What is the end result of doing these two things? He will give you peace. Put this into practice and watch peace flow into your life, and into your mind. Do these two things daily, for days and weeks to come. Put worrying to rest, and instead, pray. Let it become a first response, your initial reaction to circumstances and situations. Watch a transformation begin. I believe you will feel burdens lifted off of you and anxious thoughts become fewer. We need to be proactive in this fight instead of being only reactionary.

DAY TWENTY-FIVE

Allow me to share a portion of another poem I wrote. This one is entitled, "Be Brave."

I cannot impart bravery to you

I can encourage you, inspire you,

but it is your choice whether you will

run from Fear, or resist it

I can share with you my story

I can remind you of the battles you have fought; the victories obtained

the ground you have covered; the miles you have traversed

so that you might find a means to persist, to persevere

This poem began as a thought found in the first stanza. I have made it a goal of mine to encourage and inspire others. I realized one day, though, that I can spend time and energy investing in another, uplifting someone, but that does not mean that anything will change for him or her. I can share my story, I can read poem after poem, I can engage in one-on-one conversations, but I cannot force anyone to be brave. That is a choice each person must make. Fear is a very real enemy, but it is very adept at manipulating the situation and deceiving the intended target. It projects itself as mighty, unassailable, and immoveable, but the truth is, just as with any other demonic or spiritual foe that comes from the pit of hell, it must bow to the name of Jesus.

I realize in writing this that I can impact a number of people, maybe help them in combatting Anxiety and discovering peace, but I cannot actively or personally engage you, the reader. I cannot follow you around and make sure you are fulfilling the exercises or reading the passages or exploring the Word. That responsibility lies with you. It is a choice. You will have to decide to take up the sword and shield daily, but, the good news is that at some point, it will become second nature. The enemy will be more selective in when to engage you. Being alert, being aware of your thoughts, being mindful of God's closeness and the promises made available to you make you a formidable opponent. You can be transformed in body, soul, and spirit because of the Holy Spirit being made accessible to you through Jesus.

You have been through much, and now stand here

you could have given up, but you pressed on

I know something within is pushing you,
driving you forward

Why do you think you cannot go any further?

Why does this obstacle stand so tall in your eyes?

You have faced difficulties before

you have been beaten,

disappointed time and again

Do you find yourself standing before a new threat, a new foreboding obstacle? If so, do you feel you cannot go any further? Do you feel stuck? To reiterate the questions in the last stanza, why does this thing seem to be such a formidable obstacle? Think back to previous fights … the miles you have walked …

but did God abandon you in the midst

of those defeats, those setbacks?

Did He ever deny you assistance, or comfort?

Did He not give you access to a peace that surpasses all understanding?

Think back to those tense or unsettling moments …

What did God offer you or speak to you in those times? What brought you comfort? What caused the worries to grow still? What words or thoughts helped to quiet the doubts? Did verses or stories come to mind? Did another's testimony spark hope inside of you? Make a list below of those things. It is a good strategy to make effective weapons available to you. You are a fearsome warrior, despite what you might be feeling. The enemy wants you to think otherwise because that way he can maintain the initiative, but you are capable of more than just reacting to him, more than capable of going on the offensive. You can speak and declare happenings in the Spirit in the name of Jesus, and that action throws the enemy off; he has to react to you. So, pray, sing, praise, declare, and read the Scriptures aloud. Fill your space with life-giving words and you will not be able to hear anything spoken by the devil, as if what he had to say had any value anyhow. Speak over yourself, your loved ones, and your dreams, and watch things shift. Roots are growing down deep. Growth or change often takes place beneath the soil, out of sight. Be patient, be persistent, keep the faith, and you will experience a new mindset, a new outlook, and a new lifestyle.

DAY TWENTY-SIX

In Deuteronomy chapter 31 we read about a transition in leadership for the Israelites. Moses, knowing that he cannot take his people into the promised land, publicly announces that Joshua will be his successor in leading the nation. Moses tells the people (v. 6) that they have no reason to fear in moving forward and taking possession of the land because God is going before them. The land is occupied by foreigners, but Moses assures the Israelites that these other nations will be brought to destruction by the Lord so that they might take possession of the land He promised to give them. Moses encourages the people to be strong and courageous and reiterates the same phrase to Joshua before the multitude. He ends his speech by reminding all those present that the Lord will be with them, and that He will neither leave them nor forsake them. They should not become afraid nor discouraged because He is their ever-present help.

Time and again throughout the Old and New Testaments, God says to men and women, "Do not be afraid," or, "Be strong and courageous." Does He ask them to rely on their own strength?

What is the source of their strength? Why should they choose to be courageous? Because He is with them. He is close. He does not abandon His people. I believe that to be anxious or fearful is very much a choice. This passage in Deuteronomy implies that it is a choice. God tells the Israelites not to be afraid, but to be courageous instead. He did not tell them to act timidly, to be overcome with Anxiety. Did they have worries? I am sure they did. If they did not, I would imagine God would not have told them not to be afraid. Is it easy to be courageous? No. Will denying Fear a place of influence cause you to not experience a single worry or doubt or fearful thought? I cannot say absolutely.

As I said at the very beginning of this book, we all experience different levels of Anxiety. The solution could be a multi-faceted one. Counseling might be beneficial, a prescription may help, journaling; the list goes on and on as to what might help you in finding and holding onto peace. However, I believe we have more power in the matter than what we might think. We can say no to Fear, but will have to be adamant in that decision daily. We can monitor our thoughts and choose to shift our focus. We can either look to God or to the problem. We can talk about the issue, fret about it, or pray about it and leave it with God. God is saying the same thing to us today as He did to the Israelites thousands of years ago: Fear not! Be strong and courageous.

Let us go back to a verse I used previously that bears repeating here. Read it and repeat it to yourself. Write it out until it sinks in, until it becomes embedded in your memory. Let it emit Truth and light to your soul. Let it become nourishment for your spirit. You can stand on this verse each and every time Fear comes at you. Truth stands; it remains despite what you might feel, despite what you might see. There is power in His Word.

> *"Have I not commanded you? Be strong and courageous. Do not be afraid; do not be discouraged, for the Lord your God will be with you wherever you go"* (Joshua 1:9).

DAY TWENTY-SEVEN

Let's elaborate on yesterday's verse. We do not have to be afraid or discouraged because? Fill in the blank with your answer_______________________________________.

It says He is with us wherever we go. He is with you wherever you go. So, let's make a list. Where do you spend time through the week? In each blank below write down one location where you spend time through the week. It will be preceded by the phrase God is with me at …

1. God is with me at ___________________________.
2. God is with me at ___________________________.
3. God is with me at ___________________________.
4. God is with me at ___________________________.
5. God is with me at ___________________________.
6. God is with me at ___________________________.

Be as specific as you want. You could just say at home for one and at work for another. You can write down at the office, at the local fast food joint, a favorite restaurant, the laundromat. You can write this list on a separate piece of paper if you want. The point of the exercise is that you understand in your heart and in your soul that God is with you at all times, in all places. I need to be reminded of this too. This one thought, God is with me right now, here, in this place, will cause your perception to change; it will illuminate your reality.

DAY TWENTY-EIGHT

Let us look at another passage from the Old Testament, a remarkable happening involving the prophet Elisha and his servant. Read 2 Kings 6:8 for context. Israel is at war with Aram. The king of Aram makes plans to catch Israel off balance, to bring them to battle at a place of his choosing and defeat them. Every time, though, the Lord reveals those plans to Elisha, who then advises the king of Israel where not to go. This happens so often, and with such accuracy, that the king of Aram suspects one of his commanders to be a traitor and leaking the information to the king of Israel. When the king of Aram is informed of Elisha's role in foiling his plans, he seeks to remove him from the picture. The king sends a sizeable force by night to surround the city where Elisha and his servant are staying and capture them. When the servant awakes in the morning, he sees the encircling enemy and becomes afraid. His master's response is just the opposite.

Elisha tells his servant to not be afraid, because the enemy was far outnumbered. Surely, this confuses the servant. He knows there is no army to oppose the Arameans. He knows that it is only he and

Elisha. Elisha prays that his servant might see what he sees. The Lord opens the servant's eyes to the angelic realm and he sees a Heaven-sent army consisting of chariots and horses of fire. Elisha was not disturbed because his eyes had seen this angelic fighting force. His focus was on God, not the circumstance confronting him and his servant.

Were their lives in real danger? Most certainly. Was there a just reason to be concerned? Definitely. However, the reality of this Aramean army did not trouble Elisha because he saw the magnitude of God's provision; he saw the help that the Lord had sent. He was at peace, and in time his servant shared the same sentiment.

A favorite quote of mine that speaks on perspective comes from Pastor Bill Johnson. He states that, "Faith doesn't deny a problem's existence, it denies it a place of influence." This is not just some exercise in playing pretend. We do not just engage in wishful thinking, trying to scour the situation/circumstance/problem from our mind, and from holding our attention. We give voice to our concerns, our emotions, our doubts, and lay them before God. It is not good to bottle everything up and act pious and stoic, as if we are unmoved by an occurrence. We acknowledge the problem, but then invite God into this reality.

DAY TWENTY-NINE

What is the opposite of Fear, of being anxious? Being at peace. Peace is a difficult state of mind to obtain, and even more challenging to maintain. It is a fragile mindset, easily disrupted by external forces. An unpleasant shopping experience, an unhappy child, an unfair predicament at work, an argument, a cold … any number of things can rob you of peace. John 14:27 reminds us that Jesus has given us His peace: "I am leaving you with a gift—peace of mind and heart. And the peace I give is a gift the world cannot give. So, don't be troubled or afraid" (NLT). Jesus has given each of us a gift of peace that affects our mind and our heart. It is something that only He can give. He clearly states that it cannot come from the world. His parting words in this verse sound very similar to passages we have already examined. It is reminiscent of what He said to the Israelites under both Moses and Joshua. He encourages us today, just as He did to His disciples thousands of years ago, to not be troubled or afraid. It is a choice. Let us take the opportunity right now to pray for peace, to ask God to grant us peace.

Heavenly Father,

You are so good to me. You have repeatedly demonstrated Your goodness and faithfulness in my life, and I am thankful to be connected to You through Your Son, Jesus. He says in the book of John that He has given me a gift. I choose to receive this gift. I am troubled in my mind and in my heart. I am battling against Fear right now, trying not to become overwhelmed by circumstances. I know I do not have within myself the strength or the endurance needed to win this fight. So, I turn to You. I admit my inability to live in peace apart from You. I confess that I have turned to other venues in hopes of finding peace, of living in peace, but I realize that I can only do so with Your help. I turn over to You, all of the worries, anxious thoughts, and doubts that trouble me. I bear these burdens, but I am ready to give them up, to give them to You. I seek rest, and I know You can do this. You can calm the storms raging in me; You can quiet my mind and steady my frazzled nerves.

I ask You now, Lord, to release me from unnecessary concerns, from pestering, nagging worries, and in their place, to instill an abiding, comforting peace. You have promised in Philippians 4:7 that Your peace transcends all understanding and guards my heart and mind in Christ Jesus. Even though I do not understand it all, and why everything is happening right now; instead of succumbing to Fear,

I choose faith. I choose to believe that You are present, that You are with me, that You are aware of my situation, and that You are able to use all of this for my good. I thank You for supplying me with an unshakable, lasting, perseverant kind of peace. May it fill me up completely and drown out the worries entirely. I thank You, Lord, for Your closeness, for being attentive, and being my help in my time of need. In Jesus' name I pray, Amen.

DAY THIRTY – THE FINAL DAY

Let us return to the book of John, but this time to John 16:33, where we find Jesus addressing His disciples before He ascends to Heaven. Jesus has just explained to them that He must go in order that the Advocate (the Holy Spirit) may come. He has revealed that the world will reject them because of their faith in Him, and persecute them because they (the world) do not know Him, or His Father. He knows that they do not understand entirely what is happening and that they have questions. He encourages each of them to pray, and to ask for anything in His name, because if they do, they will receive that for which they ask. Answers to prayers will produce joy within. He paints a rather stark picture for them; their choice to follow Him comes at a cost. In His final recorded words to this group (in John's Gospel), Jesus says, "I have told you these things, so that in me you may have peace. In this world you will have trouble. But take heart! I have overcome the world" (John 16:33). What Jesus has told His disciples prior to this closing verse of the chapter is not, in large part, the most comforting, or most uplifting message, but it is truth. In verse 33 He explains why He has told them these things—that they might find peace in Him. We know that only God is capable of delivering a steadfast and lasting peace.

He reveals the difficult reality that every individual confronts—in this world we will have trouble. That is guaranteed. However, for those of us who know Jesus, we have access to a peace that surpasses all understanding. We serve a risen Savior. Jesus defeated the grave, stripped hell of all authority, and overcame the world. We have reason to celebrate! We are victors in Christ. We are, according to Romans 8:37, more than conquerors in Him. That same chapter concludes in a beautiful, soul-stirring flourish of how nothing can separate us from the love of God (v. 39). That is a truth with which we can bludgeon our fears: "I am a redeemed child of the King. I am a blood-bought son/daughter of God, and He loves me unconditionally."

What drives out all Fear? LOVE. When Fear is pressing you and driving you into despair, speak up; remind yourself that you are loved. Read Romans 8:38-39. Memorize those verses and recite them often. When Fear says you are not enough, respond with, "I am greatly and mightily loved." When Anxiety says that God has abandoned or forgotten you, respond with, "He cares deeply for me. He loves me! I am not afraid because He is right here with me." Take time to soak in this Truth. Take time in His presence. Learn the desires of His heart. Ask Him to show you who He created you to be. What does He see in you? Who does He see you becoming? What do you know of Him? How has He demonstrated His love for you in your life?

You see, when you and I know deep down inside that we are loved and adored by God Almighty, no amount of fear or distressing thoughts can take that away from us. We are powerful in Jesus. We have access to the Holy Spirit. Our words are influential. God offers us peace. We are overcomers in Christ. We have not been given a spirit of timidity. I hope you are able to take all of the pieces I have highlighted in this devotional and use them in your own struggle with Fear/Anxiety. God did not create any of us to live in constant terror, beneath the oppressive nature of Panic or Dread. He fashioned us to live freely under the lordship of Jesus Christ. Father God made us that we might enjoy a restored and intimate connection/relationship with Him in Christ.

As I said at the beginning of this journey, this book is not intended to be a program that guarantees total and complete freedom from Fear. I write this with the intention of equipping readers with tools so that they might wage a successful fight against their own worries and doubts. This is a personal war, filled with battles that many of us fight daily. It is my intention to help readers view themselves differently, to go on the offensive in their own struggle. Fear has a way of disarming people, of leaving souls feeling crushed and powerless. However, we are not incapable of bringing these storms to a rest, because we have access to God the Father through His Son, Jesus Christ. For some of you, this is just the beginning of resisting Fear, and you may want to seek out other resources, or even enroll yourself in counseling. There is no shame in seeking help, in reaching out to others. If the goal is to better ourselves, to live a life apart from Fear, then no thought should keep us in isolation. Whatever path you choose, whatever you think is best for you, I believe it ultimately will end in freedom, in being released from an over-anxious mind, sleepless nights, night-terrors, etc. Whatever is troubling you, the answer is found in Jesus. Thank you for your dedication, for the attention you gave each day, and I pray that this has proven to be helpful for you in some way. God bless!

Marty Zimmerman III (HMZ3)

PERSONAL ARMORY

Below is what I am calling your personal armory. In the space below, note verses that have helped you or will help you in combatting Anxiety. Write names or excerpts of testimonies that you find inspiring and encouraging. You can record song titles, book titles, sermons, and other resources you find that address Fear, Peace, Hope, spiritual warfare etc. You can even write down phone numbers of prayer partners, pastors, counselors, close friends—people who are committed to standing with you in this fight.

I recommend that you save a portion of the provided space to record your own testimony: those times when God arrived just in time, answered a prayer, gave you a word. Write down for your own eyes to see, so that you can remember how God moves in your life, on your behalf. Take time to note the victories and breakthroughs you already enjoy. Prepare yourself for more to come. This habit of remembering adds to your faith; it strengthens it and nourishes it. You have a counterargument to make when the lies and the disorder and the half-truths descend. You can say with confidence that God appeared here, at this moment, and that He will do it again. He is still moving, still speaking, still performing miracles. We still have a reason to be hopeful, to be joyful. Let us remember the encouragement found in Isaiah 40:31:

> "*but those who hope in the LORD will renew their strength. They will soar on wings like eagles; they will run and not grow weary, they will walk and not be faint.*"

The struggle is grueling. It is intense and it is exhausting, but if we place our hope in the Lord, He will enable us to persevere. He will give us the strength and the grace necessary to persist and to overcome.

PERSONAL ARMORY

PERSONAL ARMORY

PERSONAL ARMORY

PERSONAL ARMORY

PERSONAL ARMORY

PERSONAL ARMORY

ABOUT THE AUTHOR

Harold "Marty" Zimmerman writes to help people find hope. His purpose is to encourage others and to inspire others to persevere against whatever circumstances they face. In 2013, at the age of 25, Marty suffered and survived a hemorrhagic stroke. God preserved his life and he is grateful to still be alive. Marty is a 2010 graduate of Messiah College, and earned his M.A in Applied History in 2017 from Shippensburg University. He is also the author of *Life Interrupted: The Story of a Young Stroke Survivor*, and writes faith-based or inspired poetry and has written hundreds of poems. He is an amateur photographer, with his primary focus being landscapes. He is a student of history, and is very interested in the Civil War era. He visits the Gettysburg NMP as often as he can. He currently resides in his hometown of Greencastle, Pennsylvania.

Generation Culture Transformation
Specializing in publishing for generation culture change

Visit us online at:
www.egen.co

Write to: eGenCo
824 Tallow Hill Road
Chambersburg, PA 17202, USA
Email: info@egen.co

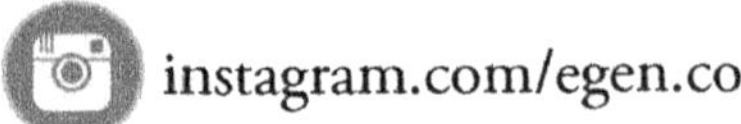